CW01390241

WORLD IN DA

PEOPLE

Steve Pollock

Illustrated by Peter Wingham

Belitha Press

First published in Great Britain in 1991 by
Belitha Press Limited
31 Newington Green, London N16 9PU

Text copyright © Steve Pollock 1991
Illustrations copyright © Peter Wingham 1991
Editor: Neil Champion

ISBN 1-85561-061-2 (hardback)
ISBN 1-85561-093-0 (paperback)

Reprinted in 1991 in Hong Kong
for Imago Publishing

Contents

People in danger

People are in danger because of what they do to their **environment**. What people do in one part of the world can affect people living in another more distant part. We are part of each other's lives and part of nature too, but we seem very quick to forget that sometimes. For example, how can eating a hamburger make a **tribe** of native Indians homeless?

The lives of all people on Earth are linked. These building blocks show how actions that take place in one part of the world affect us all . . .

It all starts by people in the **developed world** wanting cheap beef for their hamburgers. People in the **developing world** raise cattle to sell to them. To get as much cattle raised as possible, they cut down **tropical forests**. They turn land into grass because that is what the cattle eat. When the tropical forests are cut, the tribal people living in the forest lose their homes. This is the chain which links you and me to other people far across the world.

We all play a part in what we do to the environment in which we live. We are all part of the environment and nature itself. When we live in cities and we cut ourselves off from the natural world, it is very easy to think we are not part of it. We pollute the air we breathe, the water we drink, we turn the soil to desert and when we do all this, we put ourselves and other people in danger.

People have considered themselves very clever – we can solve amazing scientific problems, we can invent machines and computers to do our work and calculate for us, we can even fly to the moon. Yet how clever are we really when we ruin the Earth, the only place we have to live?

This is because the environment in which we all live is a delicate, balanced one. If we pollute the air, we pollute everybody's air . . .

If we cut down forests or dump poisons in the sea, we not only hurt the wildlife, but we hurt ourselves.

Tribal people

For thousands of years, tribal people have lived as part of the natural environment. Many live what is called a **hunter-gatherer** way of life. This means that they hunt animals, catch fish and dig for insects, such as beetle grubs or honeydew ants. Plant food in the form of nuts, berries and fruit is also gathered.

Not only can they make things from natural materials, but the plants and trees around them are a natural source of **medicines**.

Their life is not always easy, but they do not suffer from many of the diseases found in modern, developed countries.

The materials they use to make their shelters, clothes and weapons, all comes from their natural environment. Bows and arrows, **blowpipes**, even **boomerangs**, are all important for hunting.

Tribal people around the world have come under pressure to change their ways of life. For example, when they came into contact with **missionaries**, they were expected to change their religion.

People have tried to force tribal peoples from their land to take it over for their own purposes. Some **governments** have tried to stop this but many turn a blind eye. They are in favour of taming wild land and people.

Forests and jungle where tribal people live may be cleared to make new roads, provide space for farmland or even for big projects such as building a dam. New roads bring more people from the cities into the forest to find a way of life. This means less forest for the tribal peoples to live in.

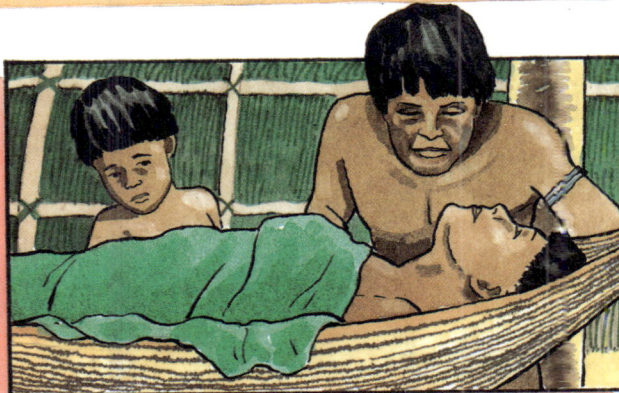

Often when outside people meet tribal people they pass on **diseases**. Chicken pox, measles and the flu do not kill people who have grown **immune** to them, but they can kill tribal people. Their bodies cannot fight these new diseases.

Many tribal people around the world have lost their homes. Many have given up their traditional lifestyles and have tried to find work in towns and cities. This is often very unsuccessful. The only hope left to them is that governments will realize that they need land and to be left to choose their way of life.

The developing world

There are many people living in the developing world. A few are rich; most are very poor. They farm the land to produce the food they need. Most of the countries are found in South America, Africa and parts of South-East Asia. There is enough land to grow the food to feed everyone. But much of the land is

People in the developing world can be at very great risk when natural disasters such as **earthquakes** happen. The buildings in which people live cannot always stand up to a large earthquake. Many of the buildings collapse.

owned by only a few people. On the land these rich people grow crops to sell for money to countries in the developed world. The kinds of crops they grow are not eaten by the people of the country but sold to developed countries.

The way people live can be dangerous. In parts of some cities there are too many people crammed into small places. There is poor drainage and clean water is hard to find. In these conditions, diseases spread quickly.

So in some of the countries in the developing world the people are forced to farm land which is poor quality. It is difficult to grow plants or find enough food for their cattle and other **livestock**.

When too many cattle eat the vegetation and wear away the soil with their **hooves**, nothing much can grow. This is made worse in years when very little rain falls. Hardly anything grows and the cattle and goats have nothing to eat and drink. They die leaving the farmers with very little.

The people have to move away to find food and somewhere to live. They become **refugees**. Sometimes other countries send extra food and medicines to help them get over these problems. But as long as they cannot find enough land to grow their food and raise their cattle on, they cannot live properly.

Without having land, some of these people move to the cities and hope they can get a job. They have no money to rent a room. So they find wood and other materials to make simple shelters. Whole towns of these shelters grow up. They are called **shanty towns**.

The developed world

The developed world contains countries that make goods such as cars, chemicals and a whole range of different **manufactured** items. They sell them to their own people and to other countries. The developed countries often take **raw materials** from developing countries. Examples of

The problem with the developed world is that it uses much more of the world's **resources** than elsewhere.

The cities in the developed world are busy and crowded. People work to earn money with which to buy goods and whatever food they need. Much of the

countries in the developed world are those in North America, Europe and in Asia, particularly Japan. We sometimes call these countries **industrialised** countries. Many of them are the richest nations in the world. By making things, they can sell them to other countries who want to buy them.

time the people in the developed world are cut off from the natural world. They are in danger from their excessive life style. They use up more than their fair share of the resources, they eat too much and they take more than they need of most things.

Most of the developed world produces waste. It is often put into holes in the ground. Waste chemicals are dumped at sea and sewage waste is put into rivers or the sea where it can cause pollution.

The way that the developed world makes its power and energy puts it in danger. Countries using nuclear power run the risk of polluting the environment. The pollution from burning **fossil fuels** can cause **acid rain** and add to **global warming**.

Many developed countries grow their food using **intensive agriculture**. This means they use extra chemicals to grow their crops and they spray them with **pesticides** too. This may cause pollution of rivers and may harm people. They may be in danger of eating chemicals in their food.

Many people in the developed world have their own car and cause pollution which creates global warming. They use valuable oil resources each time they travel somewhere.

The poverty trap

When people have their own land they can grow food for themselves. They can grow enough to trade for different foods or sell to buy what they need.

So they and their family can live their lives with enough to eat, live in a comfortable place and have all the things that people have a right to.

Understandably, people in the developing world see how the people in the developed world live. They generally have better health, more time to themselves and luxury items.

Why shouldn't they have the same? But to get these, the people in the developing world need money from the developed world to buy expensive machines for their industries, trucks and cars for transport and luxury items for themselves and their people. So crops such as coffee are grown on the land to sell abroad.

People who work in coffee plantations do not own the land. They are paid money to work. So they have to buy food with the money they earn because they cannot grow it themselves.

So the developing country gets less money. When this happens the workers get less money too. Sometimes they lose their jobs and have no money to buy food. They have little or no land on which to grow food. So the developing country needs to borrow money from the developed world to survive.

These crops are called **cash crops** because they are sold abroad for money. The money they earn from the developed world helps them buy what they need to live. In some years when a lot of coffee is grown by a lot of countries the price of coffee falls.

When this keeps happening, the developing country has to keep borrowing money. The developed world keeps lending it – this is the poverty trap.

A fair share?

There is only so much the Earth can provide. Yet we go on squeezing more and more out of it. The countries in the developed world are using up the

world's natural resources very quickly. Oil will run out in about 20 years. The more resources they use, the more goods they can make. This is called growth. The more goods they make and sell, the more money they make. The more money they make, the more rich and powerful they become.

Many of the developed countries cause pollution, make waste and use up energy when they do this, putting themselves and others at risk.

Look at the picture of the two children playing. All the things they have had to be made. They all use up part of the Earth's raw materials and some energy to make them. For some children, these things are part of their daily life. For others, they would be a luxury. For some, the hamburger and fizzy drink are the luxuries. But there is a growing fear that we are all using too much of the Earth's natural resources. Fuels, such as coal, wood, oil and gas, cannot last for ever.

Think about the world as a huge cake with all the people wanting to be given a slice. How would you share it out? Would everyone get a piece roughly the same size? The world's resources are a bit like the cake, but they are not shared out fairly.

The people in the developed world most often control the resources and they take the biggest slice, every time.

People in the developing world always get a smaller slice and it has to go further because more people live there.

The cost of a crisp

Most things in our lives have an environmental cost. Most of the time we

never think of it or even realize it. So what does it cost the environment to make a packet of crisps?

Potatoes are grown on a farm. The farmer uses pesticides, fertilizers and fuel (petrol or diesel) for energy. A lorry takes the potatoes to a factory.

The potatoes are washed, sliced and cooked. More energy is

used up and a tiny amount of pollution given off.

The crisps are then packed in bags. The material to make them is made from oil! This is a fossil fuel and once it has been used up, can never be replaced.

Once the crisps are bought and eaten, the bag is put in a bin. This is emptied and the contents either burned (causing air pollution) or

The bags are moved all over the country to shops and supermarkets for sale. More energy is used transporting them and more pollution is given off from using this energy.

buried at sea or in the ground. Crisp packets do not rot.

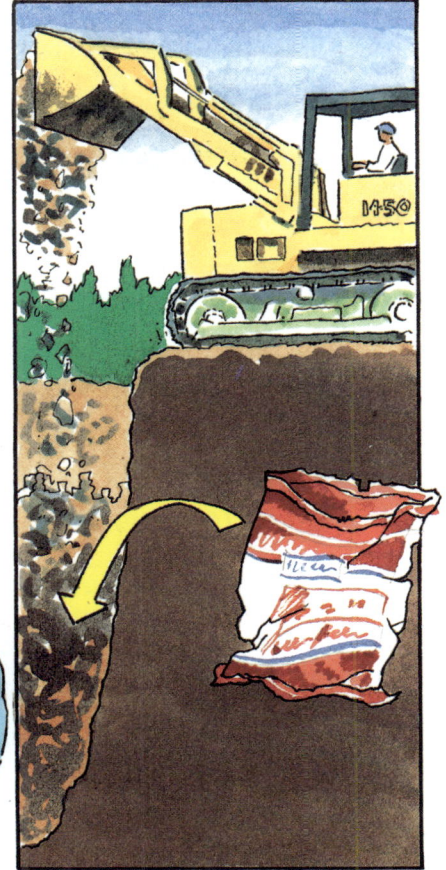

Earth's resources go into making them but they do not return to the Earth.

So everything has an environmental cost. This example is just one among many. Some things are more costly than others.

Wasting the world

In nature, everything, except the energy which comes from the sun, is renewable. Nature's raw materials go round and round in a cycle over a very long period

of time. They are recycled or they become part of something else. For example, some of the chemicals which made up the body of a dinosaur, millions of years ago, may now be part of you! Some of the chemicals may now be floating around in the air. Others might be locked up in the ground as a fossil or they may be part of a growing plant or even the metal that makes up your bike. There is only a limited amount of these materials around. Fortunately for us, they are part of the things we use but often we change them into different things. This means they sometimes cannot be put back into nature's cycle.

That's because when people use the Earth's resources they waste a great deal. Precious oil, gas and coal, which have taken millions of years to form, are burned in seconds and left to pollute the air. Oil is used to make other materials such as plastic. This is very useful but we waste it by throwing it away.

Unique **habitats** such as tropical forests which have been around for thousands of years are cut down never to be replaced.

Waste from farm animals, wh ch could be used as a natural fertilizer to grow crops, is wasted too. Because many farmers in the industrialised countries use artificial fertilizers, it is wasted. It is dumped on the land sometimes getting into rivers and causing pollution.

Some materials are used to make plastic containers and cans which we only use for ten minutes then throw away.

Global warming

When plants die, they rot down. The carbon in the plant goes back into the air. Sometimes, plants dying on swampy ground do not rot.

Much of the Earth's carbon is locked up underground as coal. Since the 1700s, people have dug coal out of the ground. When the coal is burnt, the carbon in it gets back into the air as carbon dioxide. With so much coal being burned, there is much more carbon dioxide in the air.

We breathe in the gas oxygen and breathe out the gas carbon dioxide. Dinosaurs did the same millions of years ago. In sunlight, plants do the opposite, taking in carbon dioxide and giving out oxygen. The carbon in the carbon dioxide becomes part of their stem and leaves.

Instead they gradually pile up on top of each other. Millions of years later, pressure from material that collects on top of them turns the plants into coal.

Coal and other fuels such as oil, are burned to run factories and to provide power for our homes. Carbon dioxide also gets into the air each time a car or lorry is driven. The petrol which drives the car makes exhaust fumes.

When a tropical forest is cut down and burned, more carbon dioxide gets into the air. This extra carbon dioxide adds to the Greenhouse Effect. This is caused when carbon dioxide in the air holds on to the Earth's heat. We need the Greenhouse Effect to keep the Earth from freezing. But extra carbon dioxide in the air can lead to the Earth becoming too warm. This is known as global warming.

A warmer world

As the world warms up, so the water in the oceans will expand. This is like a kettle when the water heats up ready to boil. The hotter the water, the higher up the kettle it goes.

Not only will the ocean expand but some of the ice at the North and South Poles will melt. This means extra water in the

oceans which means higher sea levels.

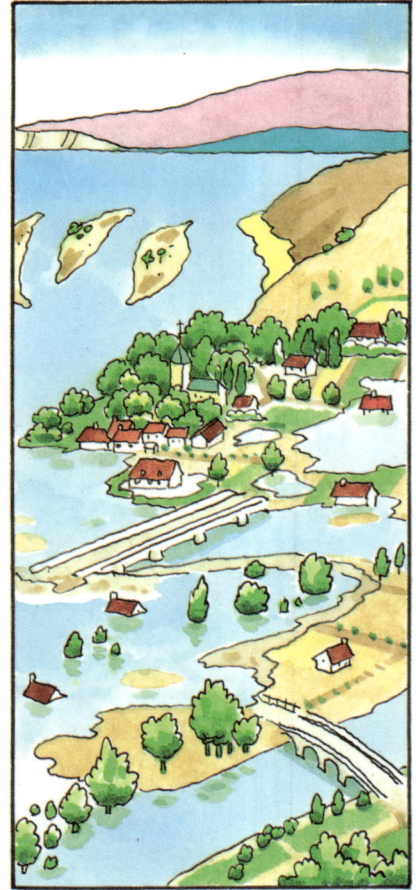

Most countries have major cities close to the seas or on rivers. Cities such as New York and London will be at risk from flooding. Part of these cities might end up under water. Whole countries, particularly low lying countries, may also be completely flooded.

Some plants will not be able to change quickly to these new conditions and may die.

The Netherlands is in danger and so is Bangladesh.

But it is not just flooding that will be a problem. In some places the warming will make fires happen more quickly. The ground will dry out.

Other plants may thrive in the new conditions. They may start to take over. This could upset nature's balance.

Some kinds of animal may do well in a warmer world but this could upset the special balance of nature. It is likely that there will be more insect pests on our crops and plants. Old ways of controlling pests might no longer work.

A problem solved?

People have always been good at solving problems. They have invented new tools and machinery to help deal with them. But there is never just one way to solve a problem. Take the

Solar panels on house roofs

problem of how to get energy. Burning oil or coal is one way. Another is to use nuclear power. Both solve the problem of getting energy but both create more problems. Burning coal and oil adds to global warming. Nuclear power makes waste materials that are very dangerous and cannot be easily thrown away. So what other ways might there be of creating energy but with fewer risks?

For countries which are quite sunny, energy from the sun might be a better way. This is called solar power. It does not cause pollution. For countries which are quite windy, modern windmills may be better. There are windmill farms around the world where energy from the wind is turned into electricity. These ways of getting energy cause no pollution. Sometimes this is called appropriate technology.

It is always possible to find different ways of solving the problem. And it is important that people choose the best one, not just to save money, but to save the environment.

Windmills making electricity

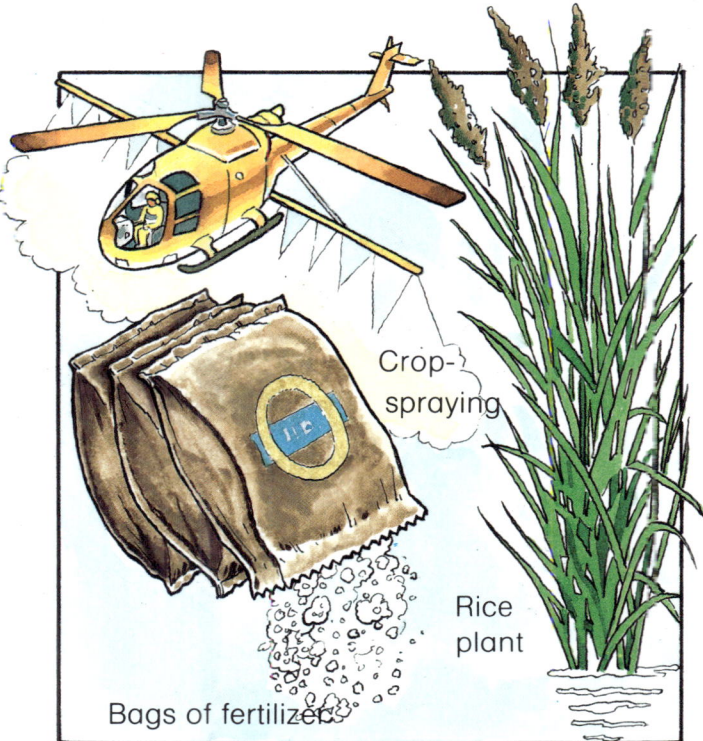

Crop-spraying

Rice plant

Bags of fertilizer

Even with extra fertilizer, pesticides and new kinds of rice, developing countries cannot grow enough food. This is because they do not have enough money to buy all of these things. A shortage of food is still putting people in danger.

It does not need to be like that. One Philippine farmer has grown more than enough food without artificial fertilizers or pesticides using a water plant called azolla. He feeds it to his pigs, ducks and chickens. Their dung and azolla are put into a biogas digester. This makes biogas which is used for heating and lighting his home. **Sludge** left over from making biogas is used as a fertilizer to grow more rice, azolla and fruit. He also farms fish which feed on azolla. This **organic farming** allows him to grow enough food to feed thirteen members of his family on a small piece of land.

Nobody need spend extra money on chemicals. Everything is natural. It is a good example of solving a problem (growing enough food) in the best way.

Azolla plant

Biogas digester

Rice

Sludge

Energy

What you can do

We all produce a lot of waste materials. It might be food we throw away. It might be old toys or clothes that we don't want any more. It might be heat and light from where we live. We make waste when we buy a bar of chocolate or a fizzy drink, when we buy things wrapped up or in a paper bag. Just think about how much effort, energy and all the Earth's resources we waste everyday. Make a list of what you do every day. Where is the waste? What can you do to reduce it?

Making a compost heap

Glass, aluminium cans, milk bottle tops – all of these are made from the Earth's precious resources. You can save energy and resources by recycling them at special collection points.

If you have a garden, you can make a compost heap as these children are doing. All the waste at meal times, including vegetable peelings, and anything else, can help to make compost.

Find interesting uses for used objects which you would normally throw away such as jam jars or other containers.

Avoid buying foods which are too highly packed. There are many different examples. A box of chocolates has so many different layers of packaging in it, all of which are thrown away.

We are so used to travelling everywhere by car. But by walking, going by bike or going by public transport you can help cut the environmental cost.

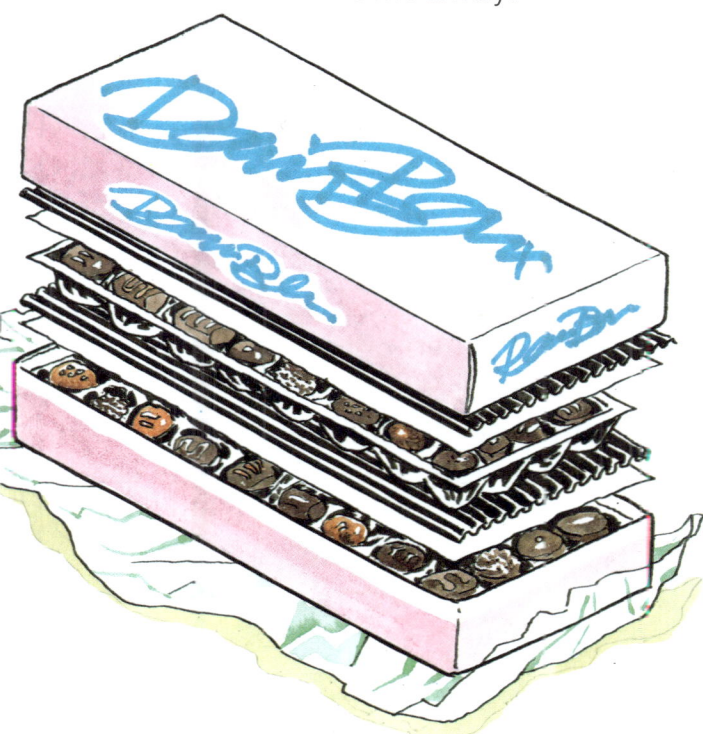

People fact file

Life expectancy
Life expectancy for countries varies a lot. In Ethiopia the average age people will reach is 42. In the USA it is 75.

Shanty town life
In the shanty town in Bangkok in Thailand, there are more than 30,000 people living as squatters in houses they built themselves.

An average of 6 people live in each dwelling, with often four to a room. Only 3 in 100 have direct access to a water supply. One in three school children do not attend school.

Our homes
About three-quarters of world housing is classed as substandard. Poor sanitation is the most serious problem.

Safe drinking water
In 1980, about 177 million people in developing world cities did not have safe drinking water and 331 million were without adequate sanitation.

The poverty trap
When a developing country grows a cash crop, it uses the cash from selling the crop to buy things it cannot make or grow itself. Oil is one thing that many developing countries have to buy from other countries.

In 1975 1 tonne of coffee (a cash crop) bought around 200 barrels of oil.

In 1983 the same tonne of coffee could buy less than 100 barrels of oil. This means less cash to buy goods from other countries. This is part of the poverty trap.

On the move
Each day in the developing world, an estimated 75,000 poor people move from the countryside to the cities. They come looking for work. They have to live in the shanty towns which build up around many cities in the developing world.

Moving to the cities
By the year 2000, half of all the world's people will live in towns and cities. In 1900 only 14 out of every hundred people lived in cities. The rest lived and worked on the land.

Money to live on

Some people in developing countries survive on an income of under £60 per year. This is what most people working full-time can earn in a day in the developed world.

Wise words

Chief Seattle (a North American Indian) said 'If men spit upon the ground, they spit on themselves. This we know – the Earth does not belong to man, man belongs to the Earth.'

Mexico City

Mexico City is probably the world's largest city. Around 19 million people live there. It is estimated that this will be around 30 million by the year 2000.

Hunger kills

Each year, 40 million people die because of hunger and its related diseases. This number is the same as if 300 jumbo jets crashed everyday and everyone on board was killed. What's worse is that almost half are children.

The world's hungry

450 million people are starving or ill-fed. 19 children per 1,000 die before the age of one in developed countries. In the developing world it is nearly five times that number – 93 children per 1,000 die before the age of one.

Energy solution?

If all the energy from the sun, the wind, water and waves could be used by people, there would never be an energy crisis. The total amount of energy given off from these sources is millions of times greater than the world's present needs.

A huge population

Over five billion (that is 5 million million) people were living in the world in 1980. More than one billion of them live in China. 700 million of them live in India. A country like Great Britain has 60 million.

Further information

There are many organisations involved with helping nature and our environment. Below are the addresses of just some of the more well known ones that you may like to contact. They may also be able to put you in touch with local organisations, if you want to get actively involved with things such as fund-raising through sponsored events. Remember, our natural world needs every friend and helper it can get!

Friends of the Earth
26-28 Underwood Street
London N1 7JQ

World Wide Fund for Nature
Panda House
Weyside Park
Godalming
Surrey GU7 1XR

Council for Environmental Education
University of Reading
London Road
Reading
Berkshire RG1 5AQ

The Save the Children Fund
Mary Datchelor House
17 Grove Lane
London SE5 8RD

Survival International
310 Edgware Road
London W2 1DY

The Conservation Trust
George Palmer Site
Northumberland Avenue
Reading
Berkshire RG2 7PW

Greenpeace
30-31 Islington Green
London N1 8XT

OXFAM
274 Banbury Road
Oxford
Oxon OX2 7DZ

The Soil Association
86-88 Colston Street
Bristol
BS1 5BB

The Centre for Alternative Technology
Llwyngwern Quarry
Machynlleth
Powys SY20 9AZ

Glossary/Index

Acid rain Rain that is mixed with polluting chemicals. It makes a weak acid and is harmful to plants and animals (11).

Blowpipe A hollow pipe used by some native Indians to shoot poisonous darts at animals (6).

Boomerang A curved weapon used by natives of Australia (Aborigines). Thrown properly, it will return to its owner (6).

Cash crop A crop grown to sell to another country for money, rather than for eating immediately (13, 28).

Developed world Countries that have developed their industries. They are the richer countries of the world. They include most countries in Western Europe, the USA and Canada, Australia, New Zealand and Japan (5, 8, 10, 11, 12, 13, 14, 15, 29).

Developing world Countries that have not developed their industries to any great extent. They rely on agriculture to feed their people (5, 8, 9, 10, 12, 13, 15, 25, 28).

Disease A disease is a particular cause of sickness. For example, measles is a disease (7, 8, 29).

Earthquake A great shaking and heaving in the Earth, caused by underground activity. Large earthquakes can cause buildings to fall and the ground to split open (8).

Environment The surrounding landscape, complete with its animals, plants, climate and soil (4, 5, 6, 16, 17, 24, 27).

Fossil fuel These are coal, oil and natural gas. They are made in the Earth or beneath the sea bed by a process of fossilisation over millions of years (11, 14, 16, 19, 24).

Global warming The belief that the world is getting warmer due to people using huge amounts of fossil fuels. This is made worse by the fact that more carbon dioxide gas is in the air and acts as a blanket, keeping the heat in (11, 20-21).

Government A group of people who control and rule over a country. There is usually a head of government, called a Prime Minister in Britain (7).

Habitat The area where a particular animal or plant lives (19).

Hooves The tough, hard part of the feet of certain animals. For example, horses have hooves (9).

Hunter-gatherers A group of people who live by hunting animals and gathering nuts, berries and fruit (6).

Immune If a person cannot catch a certain disease or sickness, they are said to be immune from it (7).

Industrialised To make an area or country industrial. This can be done by building factories, ship-building yards, steel mills, mining coal and so on (10, 19).

Intensive agriculture A type of agriculture needing few people and lots of energy and chemicals to make it work (11).

Livestock The animals kept on a farm. They may include sheep, cows and pigs (9).

Manufactured Something that has been made in a factory or by some other form of business (10).

Medicine Something used to help treat sickness and disease (6, 9).

Missionary A person sent to a place or country to teach the people about their religion (6).

Organic farming A type of farming that uses only natural things to help grow crops and feed animals (25).

Pesticide Something that is used in farming to kill pests. Pests can be insects or fungus that eat plants or harm livestock (11, 16, 25).

Raw material Materials taken straight from the Earth and before they are changed into something else. For example, iron ore is a raw material from which we get steel (10, 14, 18).

Refugee Someone who has been forced to run away from their home or country (9).

Resources The materials we use to provide us with energy (coal, oil, gas) and the means to build (wood, rocks) (10, 14, 15, 17, 19, 26).

Shanty town A disorganised, unplanned town. They are built on the edges of existing cities, by people in poor countries looking for work (9, 2, 8).

Sludge A soft muddy mixture, formed from sewage (25).

Tribe A group of people living and working together in an ancient and traditional way. They generally claim to be related to each other (4, 5, 6-7).

Tropical forest Forests found in hot, steamy parts of the world (5, 7, 19, 21).